This book is dedicated to my beautiful granddaughter Journee. You inspire me to be a better person each and every day.

Love you more than life.

Pa

Journee

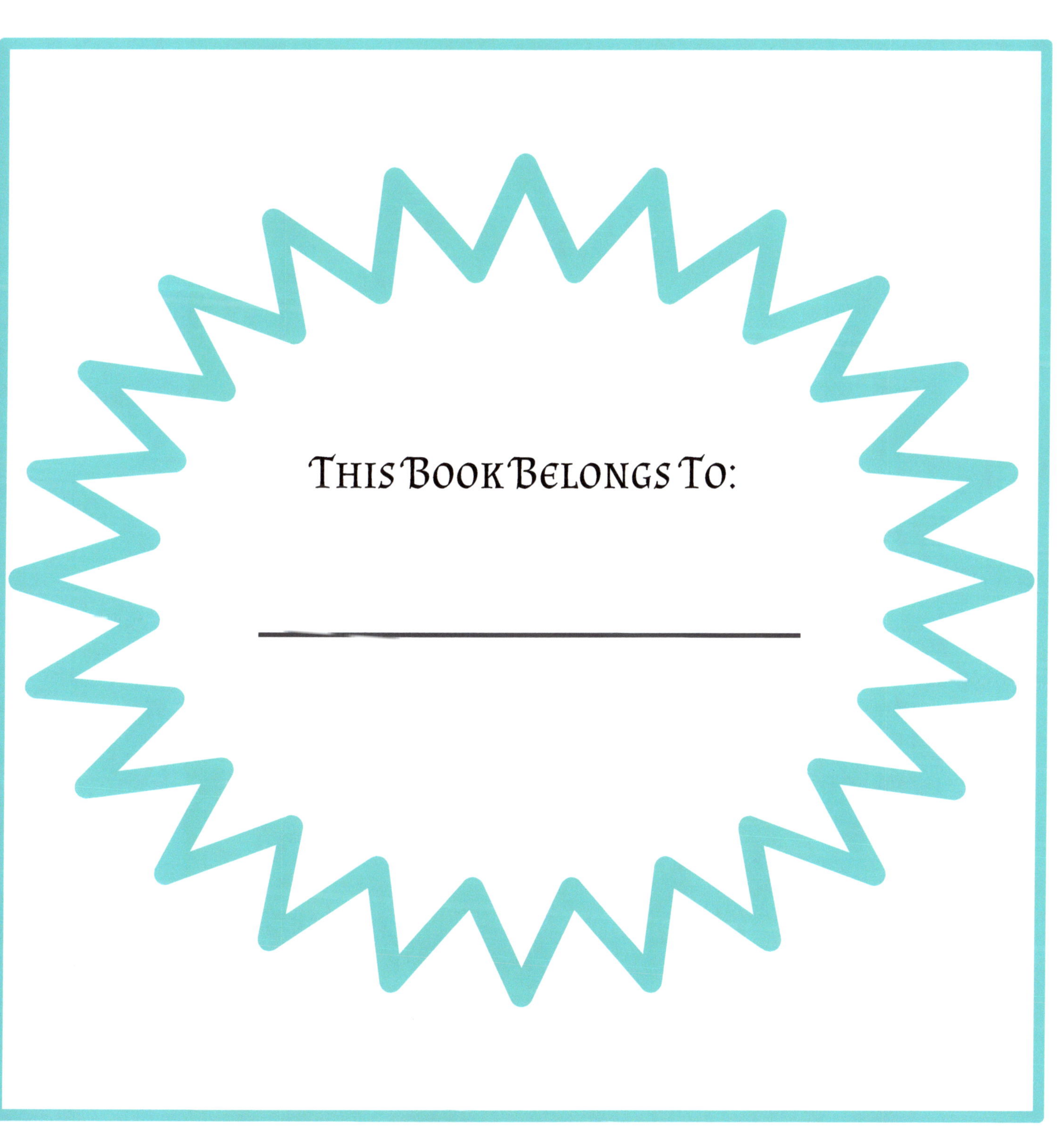

This Book Belongs To:

Journee knows that the color and shape below is

A red heart

Journee knows that the color and shape below is

A blue circle

Journee knows that the color and shape below is

A green square

Journee knows that the color and shape below is

A orange diamond

Journee knows that the color and shape below is

A yellow triangle

Journee knows that the color and shape below is

A purple rectangle

Journee knows that the color and shape below is

A gray hexagon

Journee knows that the color and shape below is

A pink pentagon

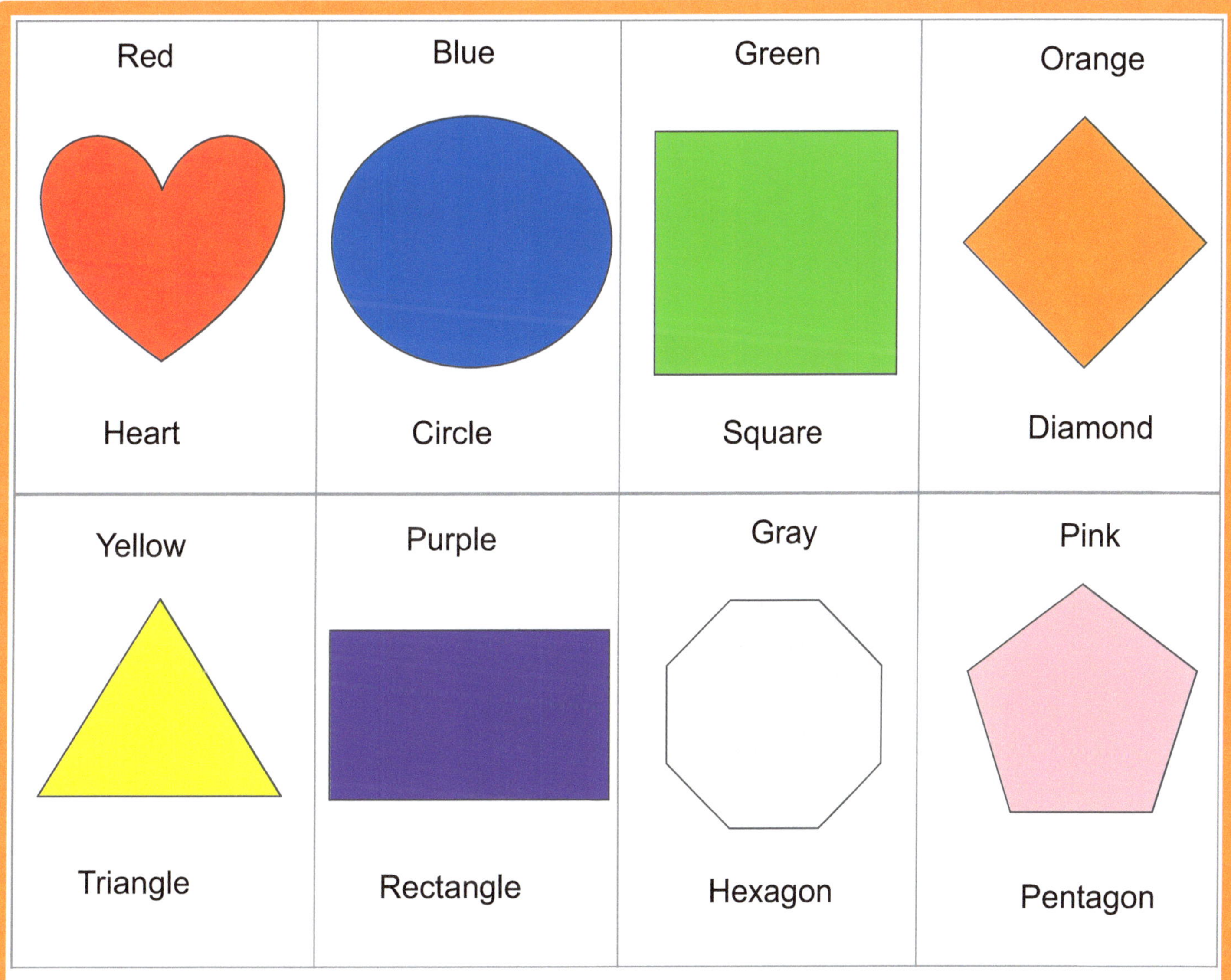

Journee's
color and shape review

Journee knows alot about colors and shapes

Now, you do too.

Stay tuned for more Journee knows adventures.